A UKRAINIAN CHRISTMAS

A UKRAINIAN
CHRISTMAS

by Nadiyka Gerbish and Yaroslav Hrytsak

Translated by Marta Gosovska
and Anastasiya Fehér

SPHERE

SPHERE

First published in Ukraine in 2020 by Portal Books under the title *The Great Christmas Book*
This translated and abridged English edition under the title
A Ukrainian Christmas first published in 2022 by Sphere

3 5 7 9 10 8 6 4

A CIP catalogue record for this book is available from the British Library.

ISBN 978-1-4087-2841-3

Printed and bound by Bell & Bain Ltd, Glasgow

Papers used by Little, Brown Book Group are from well-managed forests and other responsible sources.

Sphere
An imprint of
Little, Brown Book Group
Carmelite House,
50 Victoria Embankment
London EC4Y 0DZ

An Hachette UK Company
www.hachette.co.uk

www.littlebrown.co.uk

The publisher is making a donation to the Disasters Emergency Committee Ukraine Humanitarian Appeal on publication of this book.

In memory of Artem Dymyd
(1995–2022)
and other children of Rachel
murdered by the modern-day Herod

Contents

Foreword

The book you are holding in your hands was published in Ukraine a year before the onset of the full-scale Russia–Ukraine war. This war has been described in different ways, but here is the definition we offer: the country where Christmas is one of the most significant holidays of the year and is celebrated twice, honoring both Eastern and Western traditions, was attacked by the country where Christmas has lost all meaning.

The popularity of Christmas in Ukraine is evidenced by the fact that St Nicholas Day is a favourite holiday amongst Ukrainian children, and one of the gems of world culture is the Ukrainian Christmas song known as 'Carol of the Bells'.

Ukraine is a nation where the traditions of house-to-house carolling and *vertep* shows (nativity plays) are still very much alive. The boundaries of this *vertep*-carolling territory in the east more-or-less coincide with the Russian–Ukrainian border (*see* 'Songs and Carols', page 43). This does not mean that there are no carols in Russia. But the so-called Russian carols are either more recent works written in the late nineteenth century, or ancient Ukrainian carols appropriated by Russia. And you won't find a crowd of carollers in Russia striding the streets of a village or town on Christmas Eve, as Nikolai Gogol describes in his renowned collection of short stories called *Evenings on a Farm Near Dikanka*, or as seen in modern Lviv in the west, Kyiv in the center, and Kharkiv in the east. *Vertep* shows share the same story. If traces of them can be found in Russian culture, they were brought there by Ukrainian or Belarusian peasants who, before the First World War, fled to Siberia or far eastern Russia in search of free land to feed their families (*see* 'Vertep: The Nativity Scene', page 65).

The simple reason for it is this: both carols and nativity scenes are part of Western Christian culture, originating in the Middle Ages as a result of the Catholic Church wanting to convey the meaning of the gospels to the illiterate community. Ukrainian lands are a borderland territory for Christianity: Ukraine is the West for Eastern Christianity and the East for Western Christianity. Until the beginning of the First World War, Western Christian culture met daily with Eastern Christian culture in Ukraine, and this continued in the western part of Ukraine until the Second World War.

These encounters were marked by conflicts, sometimes terribly bloodstained, as in the Polish–Ukrainian wars of the seventeenth or twentieth centuries. On the other hand, they led to cultural exchanges and mutual borrowing. The history of the Ukrainian carol 'Ne Plach, Rakhyle' ('Don't Weep, Rachel') is especially poignant when seen in this light. Its melody is a variant of the Portuguese–Spanish folio in a musical arrangement by Arcangelo Corelli (1653–1713). The furthest point where it was recorded by the folklorists is Irkutsk, where it arrived with the forcibly displaced Ukrainians. The lyrics of this carol, in their own way, tell the modern history of the Russia–Ukraine war: Ukrainian children are dying due to 'Love for Ukraine – is all their fault, all their fault.'

Many Ukrainian carols have a distinct trace of sadness to them. Even the traditional Christmas fast, unlike Advent, is spent in abstaining, prayer and contemplation (*see* 'Feasting and Fasting', page 29). Likewise, Ukrainian Christmas Eve dinner traditions are focused on commemorating deceased family members, gratitude for being alive and together as a family, and expressing hope for a rich harvest in the coming year. As an agricultural society, Ukrainians have always depended on the crops from their fields to survive.

After Holodomor – the series of man-made famines in Ukraine organised by the Soviet regime in 1932–3 – the sacredness of bread has become deeply ingrained in Ukrainian history and day-to-day customs. The habit of raising and respectfully kissing any piece of bread that falls to the ground required by the older generation has lost its mandatory status in recent years. However, after the Russian occupation of Bucha and Mariupol in March 2022, when the bodies of starved-to-death mothers and children were buried in the yards of their own homes, perhaps the customs of earlier days might be recalled to honour and preserve the memory of present-day martyrs. And as the minefields in the de-occupied regions are slowly turned back into fields sown with wheat, maybe the old tradition of bringing supper to one's nearest family and friends as a Christmas gift might return once again. Two main dishes on Ukrainian Christmas Eve are *Kutia* and *Uzvar* (*see* pages 37–39). *Kutia* symbolises death and *Uzvar* birth and life. The essential message of Christmas and Christianity is this: death doesn't have the final word – life is eternal.

Long before the 2022 escalation, there had been a heated discussion in Ukraine about who should bring the gifts to children for the Christmas and New Year holidays: St Nicholas or Grandfather Frost, the latter being a Russian tradition. Many Ukrainians, with their inherent pragmatism, tried to reconcile the two by celebrating two Christmases, with Ukrainian children receiving gifts twice (*see* 'St Nicholas and Grandfather Frost', page 89). Yet Russian children were deprived of this prospect, not by their own choice or by the choice

of their parents, but on the whim of the Soviet regime. In the Soviet Union, not only was Christmas cancelled, but New Year celebrations were banned for a time, and pre-school children were even hauled out to watch the demonstrations against their parents holding New Year's parties (*see* 'A Ban on Christmas', page 103).

The ban on Christmas in the USSR, which lasted until the end of the Soviet Union in 1991, was very similar to what was going on in Germany under Hitler, and if in Soviet history there was only one instance when carols were sung openly and uncensored from the concert hall stage, it was thanks to a Ukrainian, Ivan Kozlovsky – said to be Stalin's favourite singer.

Ukrainian Christmas traditions, music and culture are deeply rooted in the country's history of sorrow, courage and resistance. This is not so different from the very first Christmas. Then, Judea was under occupation and the emperor's myrmidon, Herod, was a terrorist and mass-murderer, hunting innocent children to secure his own throne. Baby Jesus, Mary and Joseph had to escape to Egypt in the middle of the night and stay there for several years as refugees. As C. S. Lewis put

it, our whole world is enemy-occupied territory and Christmas is the story of the rightful king, who landed in the disguise of a child to invite us to participate in a great campaign of sabotage.

The war between Ukraine and Russia is also a war for the freedom of Christmas culture. Christmas, especially during wartime, can make the impossible happen. Enemies on both front lines can reconcile for a short time and although examples of military Christmas reconciliations might be rare, the fact they have happened gives us hope and the chance to imagine peace (*see* 'Christmas Truces', page 115). They encourage us to be optimistic that these one-time military truces might have a lasting effect after the war, but only if those modern-day Herods – Hitler, Stalin, Putin – disappear for good.

Christmas is a time that reminds us that justice and love prevail, even when it seems that both are slowly dying. It ensures the indestructibility of hope in times of the greatest hopelessness. For as long as we celebrate Christmas, we can neither be defeated nor destroyed. This is the message that Ukraine is trying to convey to the world, and this is what our book is about.

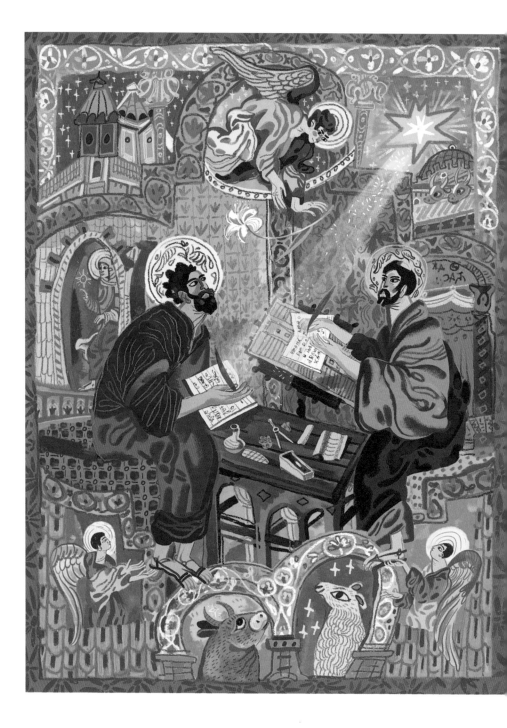

When is Christmas?

Christmas in Ukraine is celebrated twice – on 25 December and 7 January – following both Western and Eastern traditions. Over the years, there has been an ongoing discussion as to which of these dates should be used for the celebration. But considering the richness and diversity of Ukraine's cultural heritage, a consensus was reached in 2017 to celebrate Christmas twice a year – and in so doing, reconcile and enrich the traditions of Western and Eastern Christianity.

Two of the gospels – Luke and Matthew – tell us about Christ's birth, but neither of them gives us a date for it. The first person who tried to specify the year was a monk called Dionysius Exiguus (Dionysius the Humble). It was his idea to create a dating system starting from the birth of Christ. He believed that Christ was born in the thirty-first year of the reign of the Roman emperor Augustus, because that was the year of the census. It's likely that he was mistaken though because the New Testament tells us that Jesus was born during King Herod's reign, and we know that Herod died in 4 BC. So most contemporary scholars believe that Christ's birth must have taken place somewhere between 6 and 2 BC.

There is also uncertainty about the day and month of Christ's birth. The early Christians, in the second to fourth centuries, gave different dates for the nativity: 25 or 28 March; 9 or 31 April; 21 May; 17 or 28 November; 25 or 28 December. The date of 25 December was calculated by St Cyprian, bishop of Carthage (born in 258), and over time this date was celebrated.

Interestingly enough, Christmas wasn't celebrated until the third century. Instead, the first Christians celebrated only the Resurrection of Jesus Christ at Easter, believing this to be the key event that gave the entire Christian story its meaning.

These early Christians considered a birthday to be a purely pagan holiday. One of the first Church Fathers, Origen (185–253/4), referenced the words of the prophet Jeremiah: 'Cursed be the day I was born! May the day my mother bore me not be blessed!' (Jeremiah 20:14). Origen reminded Christians that no saint commemorated his birthday. What's more, he claimed that they cursed the day they had been born.

But another important factor played a role in Easter taking precedence over Christmas in the early Christian calendar: in the Roman Empire, Christians were considered state criminals. They were routinely persecuted and subjected to torture and martyrdom. Under such circumstances, placing the emphasis on Christ's death and resurrection was very natural. They believed that both saints and martyrs should be remembered on the day of their death – their true birth for eternity. They also anticipated that the second coming of the Messiah would occur during their lifetimes.

All this changed when Constantine, who had come to power as Roman emperor in 306, fought a battle against the Emperor Maxentius. The battle took place on the outskirts of the city, next to the Milvian Bridge over the Tiber River. Constantine's chances of victory were slim: his army was fatigued by the long trek and began surrendering in great numbers. However, that night Constantine had a dream. He saw the sign of the cross in the sky and heard the words, 'In this sign, you will conquer'. In the morning he commanded his soldiers to paint crosses on their shields and by the end of the day his army had won the battle.

A few different versions of this story exist. Nevertheless, they all agree that the victory at the Battle of the Milvian Bridge in 312 marked the beginning of Constantine's conversion to Christianity. He legalised Christianity and it soon became the official religion of the Roman Empire. Unsurprisingly, the first written reference to the celebration of Christmas dates from the time of Constantine's reign. It is found in the Roman Chronograph of 354 and cites the year 336 as the date for the first celebration of Christmas.

There was another event in Constantine's reign that would have worldwide significance. He relocated the capital from Rome – which was under the constant threat of the Barbarians – to Byzantium, a Greek colony on the coast of the Black Sea. Here, he built a new city, Constantinople, which was well protected on all sides by a mountain range and the sea. A new empire was formed, with its capital in Constantinople, which eventually became known as the Byzantine Empire – and this was the main territory in which Christmas was officially celebrated every year.

In 476, under the onslaught of the Barbarians, Rome finally and definitively fell, and the lands of the former Roman Empire were plunged into the Dark Ages (500–800), a period of unremitting wars and decline.

All the Eastern Christian Churches, with the exception of the Armenian Church, accepted 25 December as Christmas Day. In contrast, Christians in Egypt celebrated Christmas on 6 January – the day in which the Three Wise Men from the East visited Christ,

the Virgin Mary and Joseph, and presented them with gifts. This date was also associated with the baptism of Jesus, which in most Western Churches is known as the Epiphany.

Hence, a situation arose where the Eastern and Western Churches celebrated Christmas on different days. So in 567, the Council of Tours came to a constructive compromise, introducing Christmas holidays that lasted for twelve days, from 25 December to 6 January. Within the next few centuries, different cultures introduced additional celebrations on Epiphany Eve, Twelfth Night. In Britain, this was a time of general merriment (and is where the name of the Shakespeare play *Twelfth Night* comes from). In the eastern Orthodox countries, it is the night of the second Holy Supper.

Christianity came to England in the seventh century and to Germany in the eighth century, but it was neither completely nor definitively established in these countries during the Dark Ages. Christian missionaries continued to perish at the hands of pagans, as was the fate of St Boniface, who brought Christianity and the symbol of the Christmas tree to Germany. It was also the fate of another great martyr, Václav, who formed the basis of the English carol about 'Good King Wenceslas' of Bohemia (the present-day Czech Republic).

The coronation of the Frankish King Charlemagne as the emperor of the new Holy Roman Empire proved to be a turning point. It was held in Rome on Christmas Day of 800, and Charlemagne accepted the imperial crown from the hands of the Pope. Since then, Christmas has been an official holiday in the lands that were part of this large empire: present-day France, Germany and Northern Italy. Then, Christmas gradually arrived in eastern and northern Europe with the Christianisation of Moravia (863), Bulgaria (864), Poland (966), Rus (988), Hungary (1000), Sweden (1100), Norway (1154) and Lithuania (1387).

In its early stages, the Christian Christmas was superimposed on existing pagan traditions almost everywhere. The Church didn't simply repress or eradicate these traditions, but cleverly utilised them and adapted them to its goals. Pope Gregory the Great officially approved this tactic. He recommended not destroying the pagan temples, but only the idols in them, and replacing them with Christian symbols. That, he wrote, is what God had done with the Jewish people in Egypt and what Paul the Apostle had done in Greece.

It's perhaps no surprise that Christmas day, on 25 December, falls on one of the shortest days of the year. To bring a bit of life-affirming light during this difficult and dismal period, the non-Christian peoples would hold midwinter holidays, or festivals. The most well-known of these was *Yule* (mid-November–early January) in Northern Europe, *Saturnalia* (17–24 December) and *Kalenda* (from 1 January as the beginning of the new year; hence the words 'calendar' and '*kolyadky*', as Christmas carols are called in Eastern Europe) in Rome. And so, in the middle of the gloomy and cold winter, when the ground was frozen and people were suffering from malnutrition and a multitude of ailments, some joyous days appeared.

These were the happiest of holidays, when work would stop, tables would bow under the weight of food and people would decorate their houses with branches and candles, visit one another, exchange gifts, organise carnivals and devote themselves to merrymaking in every imaginable way. A similar tradition even existed among the Barbarian peoples north of the Roman Empire. They followed the solar calendar and, accordingly, celebrated the summer (21 June) and winter (21 December) solstices.

In Ancient Egypt, celebrations fell on 6 January. This concluded the obligatory forty days of fasting which marked the death of Osiris. It was believed that on the fortieth day, when Osiris rose from the dead,

the waters of the Nile turned into wine, and bathing in the river marked the end of the fasting.

Christians consciously adopted not only certain traditions from non-Christians, but also the date of their celebrations, helping to lend them religious significance and convey the joy of Christ's birth. Ancient theologians also believed that God had created the world at the beginning of spring, on 25 March. Accordingly, his son – Jesus – was supposed to be conceived on that same day, and the end of the ninth month of pregnancy fell on 25 December.

By the end of the sixteenth century a new schism emerged between Western and Eastern Christians in the celebration of Christmas, due to the introduction of a new calendar. The old Julian calendar was lagging behind the solar cycle because the astronomical year doesn't last precisely 365 days – but 365 days, 5 hours, 48 minutes and 6 seconds. Despite adding a leap year every four years, the Julian calendar gradually fell out of sync with the equinoxes – and equinoxes were vital for calculating Easter correctly. Pope Gregory XIII decided to drop ten days to bring the calendar back into line with the equinoxes. This became known as the Gregorian calendar.

The Orthodox churches did not accept these reforms and stuck to the Julian calendar. By that token, what was the end of December for Western Christians became the beginning of January for Eastern Christians. The gap grew with every century, and there is now a difference of thirteen days. Therefore, Christmas in Ukraine lasts from 7–18 January (in 2017, Ukraine recognised 25 December as an official holiday, along with the traditional Orthodox Christmas on 7 January). Nowadays, Ukraine together with Belarus, Eritrea, Lebanon and Moldova are the countries where Christmas comes not once, but twice a year.

Ukraine's traditions reflect the syncretic nature of Christmas. Christmas emerged as a holiday in the Mediterranean and spread through the lands of the western and eastern (Byzantine) Roman Empires to the 'Barbarian' lands of northern Europe. With the rise of Europe since the sixteenth century, and its transformation into a world power, Christmas has gradually spanned the world, absorbing local traditions and transporting them to other territories. Christmas has continued acquiring one thing and losing another to the point where it has now become a truly global holiday, the most well-known in the world.

Feasting and Fasting

In the four Sundays leading up to Christmas, churches in the Western tradition celebrate Advent. It is a time for reflection and preparation for the celebration of Christ's birth. In contrast, Ukrainian Orthodox and Greek-Catholic churches' traditions observe not Advent, but *Pylypivka*, or St Philip's Fast, which begins on the day following the feast of the apostle St Philip.

The Christmas Fast is one of the four main annual fasts in the Eastern Christian calendar. Like Advent, it is a period of preparation when, by showing restraint in food and entertainment, Christians prepare their hearts for Christmas through repentance and prayer.

Christmas fasting began in the fourth century and, at first, the fast only lasted seven days. But at the Council of 1166, held under the Patriarch of Constantinople, Luke and the Byzantine emperor, Manuel, a decision was made to extend the fast to forty days before Christmas.

The number forty occurs repeatedly in the Bible as a symbol of testing and hardship. For example, Moses and the Israelites walked in the desert for forty years, Jesus fasted in the desert for forty days and, after the resurrection, he appeared to the disciples for forty days before the Ascension.

Hence, in Ukraine today the Christmas Fast begins on 28 November and lasts until 6 January according to the Gregorian calendar (or 15 November until 24 December according to the Julian calendar). During this time, Christian believers follow a kind of vegan diet: no animal products are permitted (although on certain days fish is allowed) and the meals consist mainly of vegetables, porridge, beans and mushrooms. It is also forbidden to dance, sing or organise parties, including weddings. In fact, the only rite allowed during the Christmas fast is baptism.

This is a time for the preparation of one's own heart: a time when entertainment is replaced by silent prayer and sincere forgiveness, and when singing gives way to gentle conversation. It is an opportunity to shelter from the noise and distractions of the outside world and focus on what is important, drawing strength and joy from the anticipation of Christmas.

On the last day of the Christmas fast, 6 January, it is customary to commemorate the hardships of Mary and Joseph's journey to

Bethlehem by not eating anything until the first star appears in the sky. If the winter is snowy, children, who are allowed only a light snack, go sledging until they notice the first star. They then rush home, with cheeks red from the frost and fun, full of excitement for Christmas Eve.

In general, food plays a special role in the Bible. The most awe-inspiring New Testament stories mention food as a symbol of fellowship, care and even miracles: Jesus feeds the five thousand; Jesus shares the Last Supper with the disciples; Jesus prepares breakfast for weary disciples on the shores of Lake Tiberias after his resurrection.

Dinner on Christmas Eve is known as the Holy Supper. It is a symbol of communion and care for each other, with the whole family gathered around one table, and meals served not as individual portions, but placed in the middle of the table in painted earthenware dishes and passed around to each other with a smile.

This is the last day of the Christmas fast, so all meals on Christmas Eve are prepared from foods without dairy products and meat. There should be twelve dishes on the table. This number, too, is symbolic: the twelve months in a year, the twelve tribes of Israel, the twelve apostles.

There is no mandatory list of dishes, but, traditionally, there should be *kutia* (*see* page 37), *uzvar* (*see* page 39) and pastries on the table. Some other dishes traditionally prepared are *borsch* with dumplings (*see* page 40), or mushroom soup (from porcini mushrooms), (*see* page 41); *varenyky* (half-moon shaped dumplings) stuffed with potatoes or stewed cabbage; *holubtsi* (cabbage rolls), pickled herring, roasted carp, stewed beans, *pampushkas* (buns), *tushkovana kapusta* (stewed cabbage with mushrooms) and jellied fish.

The roots of Ukrainian Christmas Eve traditions are often intermingled: some originate in the pagan customs of people living off the land, and others are based on Christian rituals. On a table covered with an embroidered tablecloth, there will be one plate more than there are people in the house. This ritual is observed in memory of deceased relatives, but it also serves as an invitation to any lonely strangers who might pass by the house in need of shelter and community. The floor is covered with hay as a reminder of the humble conditions in which Jesus was born.

There is a lavish variety of recipes for even the most traditional dishes. Ukraine, covering approximately 600,000 square kilometers, is a beautiful patchwork of different backgrounds. The traditional *kutia* is made with wheat. However, in some eastern regions *kutia* is cooked with rice. Ukrainian writer Lyuba Yakimchuk, originally from the Luhansk region, says that *kutia* in her parent's house was made with round, crumbly rice. They used to add poppy seeds, raisins and honey. Now that same house is under occupation.

'Prayer' by Lyuba Yakimchuk

Our Father, who art in heaven
of the full moon
and the hollow sun
shield from death my parents
whose house stands in the line of fire
and who won't abandon it
like a tomb
our daily bread give to the hungry
and let them stop devouring one another
and forgive us our destroyed cities
even though we do not forgive for them our enemies
shield and protect
my husband, my parents
my child and my Motherland

This was the poem Lyuba Yakimchuk read from her book *Apricots of Donbas* at the 64th Grammy Awards ceremony on 3 April 2022, as American singer John Legend sang his song 'Free' with Ukrainian singer Mika Newton. Lyuba says that she cooks wheat *kutia* now, celebrating the cultural diversity of Ukraine, but her mother still opts for the rice version.

Whatever the differences, Ukrainian dishes, especially for Christmas Eve, are organic, made from scratch, have rich flour, a

deeply rooted history and, more often than not, a symbolic meaning or two. By the way, the unmarried girls in the family are forbidden to lick the *makohin* (wooden pestle), used to crush the poppy seeds in the *makitra* (a big clay mixing bowl, usually handmade). There is a superstition that if a girl licks the poppies from the *makohin*, her future husband will be bald. Most girls don't care!

Here we share two different recipes of *kutia* – one from wheat and the other from rice, coming from the western and eastern regions of Ukraine, respectively – *uzvar*, Ukrainian vegetable *borsch* with mushrooms and Carpathian mushroom soup. Each recipe is designed to serve a family as part of the Christmas Eve Holy Supper of twelve dishes.

Smachnoho (bon appetite)!

Traditional Wheat Kutia
(Christmas wheat berry pudding)

INGREDIENTS:

200g wheat kernels*

600ml water

100g raisins

100g poppy seeds

100g chopped nuts

  (e.g. flaked almonds,

  walnuts)

2–3 tbsp honey

Wheat kernels, also called wheat berries, can be found in organic and Asian food stores, or pearl barley can be used as an alternative.

METHOD:

1. Rinse the wheat kernels and soak them for at least 4 hours or overnight.

2. Drain and cover the soaked grains with the measured water and simmer a on low heat for 2–3 hours, until cooked. The wheat should be soft but not overboiled. Add some boiling water during cooking if it begins to look dry.

3. Cover the raisins with warm water and leave to soak for half an hour.

4. Meanwhile, grind the poppy seeds using the *makohin*, or a pestle and mortar, and chop the nuts.

5. Combine the wheat kernels, poppy seeds, raisins and nuts in a *makitra* or a casserole dish. Add honey to taste and mix together.

6. Allow to cool before serving.

Traditional Rice Kutia

INGREDIENTS:

100g poppy seeds
50g raisins
50g walnuts
200g white rice*
120g honey
100–200ml uzvar
(see page 39) or water

*You can use any white rice, but medium or short-grain varieties are more popular.

METHOD:

1. Rinse the poppy seeds, cover with boiling water and leave to soak for an hour. Then drain and grind the poppy seeds thoroughly using a pestle and mortar.

2. Rinse the raisins and put in a bowl. Pour boiling water over to cover them and leave to soak for 30 minutes.

3. Chop the nuts and gently toast them in a pan or oven.

4. Rinse the rice and cover with water. Bring briefly to the boil and then drain and rinse with cold water.

5. Cover the rice with 600ml of water and a pinch of salt, and simmer for approximately 15 minutes or until cooked.

6. Mix the honey with the uzvar or water.

7. Mix the cooked rice, raisins, nuts, honey mixture and salt to taste. If the kutia turns out to be thick, you can add more uzvar or water to reach the right consistency.

Traditional Uzvar

This drink is a symbol of birth and life and is wonderfully fragrant, tasty and healthy.

INGREDIENTS:

1.5 l water
a handful of dried apple
slices
a handful of dried pear
slices
1 tbsp dried rosehips
a handful of prunes
a handful of raisins
1 tbsp dried cranberries
1 tbsp dried strawberries
1 cinnamon stick
2 star anise
3 cloves
3 allspice berries
1 tbsp honey

METHOD:

1. Bring the measured water to a boil and add the dried apples, pears and rose hips. Cook for 10 minutes.

2. Then add the prunes, raisins, dried cranberries and strawberries.

3. Cook for another 10 minutes. Just before removing from the heat, add the spices.

4. Allow to cool and add the honey.

5. Infuse the uzvar for 3–4 hours in a vessel with a closed lid. It is best left overnight.

Traditional Vegetable Borsch

On 1 July 2022, Ukrainian *borsch* soup was included on Unesco's endangered cultural heritage list. The first written mention of Ukrainian *borsch* cooked in Kyiv dates back to 1584. Vinegar was added to the dish in Soviet times. Before that, beet *kvass* was generally used.

INGREDIENTS:

a handful of dried
  porcini mushrooms
300g fresh beetroot
1 medium carrot
1 onion
1 tomato
2 tbsp sunflower oil
2 tbsp vinegar
1 tsp sugar
salt and pepper
400g baking potatoes
300g white cabbage, cut
  into strips
2 bay leaves
4 cloves garlic, finely
  minced
bunch of parsley,
  chopped
bunch of dill, chopped

METHOD:

1. Add the dried mushrooms to a saucepan, cover with boiling water, then drain and rinse. Then add warm water to the mushrooms and soak for 30 minutes. Without changing the water, boil the mushrooms until softened.

2. Wash and peel the vegetables. Then, chop the onion and tomato, and grate the beetroot and carrot. Sauté the onion, carrot, beetroot and tomato in the oil. Add the vinegar, sugar and salt.

3. Dice the potatoes and add them to the mushrooms, seasoning the water with salt. Cook for 5–10 minutes, then add the cabbage. Boil for 10 minutes, then add the sautéed vegetable mixture.

4. Leave the borsch on the stove for all the vegetables to soften. Season the dish with black pepper and the bay leaves.

5. Serve the borsch with the minced garlic, chopped parsley and dill.

Carpathian Mushroom Soup

This traditional soup comes from the Carpathian mountain region in western Ukraine. Like the *borsch*, it is a vegan recipe.

INGREDIENTS:

100g dried porcini
   mushrooms
2.5l water
4 medium potatoes
1 parsley root, or parsnip
1 onion
1 carrot
1 tbsp sunflower oil
salt and pepper
2 bay leaves
3 cloves garlic, chopped
bunch of parsley,
   chopped

METHOD:

1. Soak the dried mushrooms in cold water for several hours. Rinse well and drain. Add the mushrooms to a large saucepan with the measured water, and cook for about an hour on a low heat.

2. Wash and peel the vegetables and dice the parsley root or parsnip. Dice the potatoes, roughly chop the onion and grate the carrot.

3. After the mushrooms are well cooked, add the diced potatoes and the parsley root. Sauté the onion and carrot in the oil and add to the soup.

4. Add salt, pepper and the bay leaves and cook for another 7–10 minutes. Add the chopped garlic and parsley and remove from the heat.

5. If you prefer a creamy texture, blend the soup and serve in soup cups.

Songs and Carols

Music has a special ability to create an atmosphere and transfer a feeling across space and time. For Christians, it is also the instrument through which God expresses the unspeakable, and a few chords can give us a glimpse of Paradise. No wonder the shepherds received the news of the newborn Messiah through angels singing!

The first mention of a Christmas carol dates back to 129, a time before Christmas existed as a holiday. In that year, the then-Bishop of Rome announced that 'in the Holy Night of the Nativity of our Lord and Savior, all shall solemnly sing the Angel's Hymn.' In the fourth century the first religious Christmas carols began to appear in Rome. They were written in Latin so would not have been understood by ordinary people.

In contrast, it remains a mystery when Christmas folk songs appeared. It seems plausible that they may have been based on pagan songs, not least because their names – 'carols' in English, *julmusik* in Swedish and *koliady* in Slavic languages – are associated with pagan customs. 'Carols' comes from the Greek *choros*, the name of the songs performed in a circle dance; *julmusik* from *yule*, the name given to the midwinter holiday of the Germanic people; and *koliady* probably from *calendae*, the Roman name for the midwinter holiday. According to another, less likely explanation, it comes from *Koliada*, the Slavic pagan god of winter (*see* page 8). Their pagan roots are confirmed by the fact that the oldest of these Christmas folk songs do not contain Christmas plots.

In the Ukrainian language, this type of Christmas folk song is called *shchedrivky*. There is an ongoing debate among scholars as to whether *shchedrivky* and *koliady* are two different genres or two varieties of the same genre. But it's clear that the Ukrainian people distinguished carols that were based on the gospels, and only sung in church, from those Christmas songs that were sung door-to-door, offering good wishes for a bountiful harvest, happiness and the good health of the household.

The Christian Church initially treated these folk songs with suspicion and reluctance: Christianity spread in Europe, where 'Barbaric' customs prevailed after the fall of the Roman Empire, and the Byzantine Empire and the Arab world were considered the only

cultured civilisations. So, the 'Barbaric' understanding of God at this time was close to the Old Testament one: a just but stern and punishing Father. It was God the Judge who severely punished people for their earthly sins, because how else could this disobedient Barbarian tribe be disciplined and taught morals? This is well conveyed by the medieval legend of how a priest caught men and women dancing in a churchyard. When he asked them to stop dancing they refused, and then in response to their punishment they danced non-stop until the following Christmas.

The situation changed dramatically in the twelfth century when Europe began to experience what historians would later call the 'First Renaissance'. Trade flourished, cities grew, universities appeared and, thanks to the Arabs, Christian theologians discovered the texts of Aristotle, Plato and other ancient sages. The French monk Adam of St Victor expanded the musical repertoire of the Notre Dame school, combining Latin religious poetry and well-known melodies of the time. It was then that the very nature of Christian spirituality began to change. Christian believers' relationship with God became more intimate and the idea of confession emerged. God himself was presented no longer as a punishing God, but first and foremost as a God

of love – a God who loved his people so much that for their salvation He sent to earth and sacrificed His only Son.

The embodiment of this new understanding of Christianity was St Francis of Assisi, who was also the first populariser of Christmas folk songs in Europe. The cheerful Italian monk, who loved animals, herbs and streams, believed that the Church should not imprison its hymns and choirs within the stone walls of its churches. He tried to convey the Christian message of God's love to the common, uneducated people: he chose simple Christmas songs based on gospel stories and simplified their intricate melodies. Each of these songs emphasised the message that God sent His Son to the people because of His love; that the Son of God did not descend to this world for the mighty, but for the poorest and humbled – because He was not born in a palace, but in a bare cave.

By the thirteenth century, the tradition of singing Christmas carols, not in Latin but in a language understood by the singer, had become quite common in Europe thanks to the Catholic monastic orders. Priests and poets translated the Latin texts used in the Church service into everyday language and shared them with the faithful, who gladly picked them up.

The oldest among them are the German carol (written in simple Latin) 'In Dulci Jubilo' and the Old Polish carol 'W Zlobie Lezy' ('Infant Holy, Infant Lowly'). Their lyrics retell the story of Christ's birth as written in the Gospels of Luke and Matthew. In some cases, details from the apocryphal gospels are added to this story. For example, one of the oldest English carols, 'The Cherry-Tree Carol', tells the story of

the pseudo-Matthew gospel: the Holy Family stops to rest in a cherry orchard and Mary asks Joseph to bring her cherries while she is caring for the child. Joseph is offended and angrily says that the real father of the child should get the cherries, not him. Then the cherry tree itself leans towards Mary and feeds her with its fruits, and the ashamed Joseph repents and renounces his words.

These stories are sometimes sad, sometimes funny; their heroes behave like ordinary people (Joseph quarrels with Mary), but they are always full of mystical light and human warmth. And most importantly, they carry the message that even the weakest and poorest are not left to fend for themselves.

The fifteenth to sixteenth centuries was the golden age of carols. They were sung in churches, at home and on the street. Their texts and notes were widely distributed due to the invention of the printing press, and the fact that music became a professional occupation added to their popularity. The music for the carols was written by professional composers, who often took folk melodies as a basis and gave them a more beautiful sound by moving from monophony to polyphony, so the songs were sung not by one but by several voices. Sometimes these voices sang different melodies, creating a wonderful harmony. In particular, many amazingly beautiful Christmas songs originated in England, where, in the fifteenth century, John Audelay published the first collection of *Christmas Carols*.

Christmas traditions changed in the sixteenth century with the growth of Protestantism. Protestants called for a return to the simplicity of early Christianity and sought to cleanse it of the elements of Catholicism. And since the early Christians neither celebrated Christmas nor sang carols, these traditions were discarded as part of the 'purification' process. But it was different in other countries. Martin Luther loved Christmas carols and contributed to the spread of this tradition in German Protestant communities, even writing several new carols himself. In England, Scotland and Ireland on the other hand, Oliver Cromwell vetoed the tradition of singing carols. The ban, however, did not last long and was lifted after the Puritans lost power and England became Anglican again. The ban was then revived among the Puritans who moved to North America, in those states where they were in power.

One way or another, in England and America at the beginning of the nineteenth century, it looked as though carols as a genre might soon disappear altogether. Fortunately, the risk did not last long. The authors of English Christmas carols, including John Mason Neale (scientist, poet, caretaker and Anglican priest), translated many songs from Latin and French into English. Over time, prejudices about Christmas also disappeared in the United States, where the freedom of the new land became a fertile ground for many world-famous Christmas songs.

For its part, the Catholic Church actively used church carols as a weapon in the fight against Protestantism. Protestantism had won its supporters by carrying the Word of God directly to the common people in a language they understood. To win over the Protestants, the Catholic elite translated carols from Latin into local languages.

From the Catholic world, the carolling tradition passed to the Orthodox world. In 1596, part of the Orthodox Polish–Lithuanian Commonwealth accepted a union with Rome. Along with this union came the custom of singing Christmas songs based on gospel stories. In some cases, these were almost literal translations. For example, the Latin anthem of the sixth and seventh centuries, 'Angelus pastoribus dixit vigilantibus', was translated in the sixteenth and seventeenth centuries first into Polish and then into Ukrainian under the name 'The Angel Spoke to the Shepherds'.

Most of the carols we know today, however, are not translations but original works. They are overgrown with new plots and images, which were not, and could not have been, in the Latin church hymns because they reflect the circumstances of the lives of ordinary people in Germany and neighboring lands. In folk carols, Christ is born in winter among the frosts and, together with Mary and Joseph, suffers from the cold. Special emphasis is placed on the poverty of the Holy Family. They can't find a place to sleep, they are driven away like beggars and not allowed into the houses, until the poorest innkeeper takes them into his stable.

Similarly, Jesus, Mary and Joseph themselves are depicted not as Judean, but as representatives of local European nations, as if Christmas took place not in Judea, but in German, Polish, Czech or Belarusian and Ukrainian lands. This same domestication of Christmas and its stories took place in other continents with the spread of Christianity. In the Argentine carol, 'La Peregrinación', Joseph and Mary do not

travel through the desert, but through the Argentine pampas. In this way, carols as a genre quickly became nationalised, retelling the gospel stories in their own way and adding local details. Almost every national culture has its own carols.

A question remains about whether Russian church carols ever existed. Those Russian carols that we know are either *shchedrivky* or works of Russian high art culture of the nineteenth century. What are known in the West as Russian carols, for example 'A New Joy has Come' are often, in fact, Ukrainian carols, as one can tell simply by listening to the language they are performed in. In any case, the border between the Kyiv and Moscow Orthodox traditions largely coincides with the border between the territory where people know and sing Christmas songs, and the territory where they are unknown and unsung.

In some cases, carols can be found across the world containing political themes. Some may end with wishes for a whole nation to free themselves from the yoke of another and regain their freedom. For example, 'The Coventry Carol' from England and 'Ne Plach, Rakhyle' ('Don't Weep, Rachel') from Ukraine are two carols to have come to life during wartime.

They are both based on the Old Testament story of Rachel, wife of Jacob, the mother of Joseph, from the Book of Jeremiah. Rachel, as the original mother of the Jews, cries for her children who were taken captive by the Assyrians. In the New Testament, Matthew connects this story with the killing of infants on Herod's orders:

'When Herod realised that he had been outwitted by the Magi, he was furious, and he gave orders to kill all the boys in Bethlehem and its vicinity who were two years old and under, in accordance with the time he had learned from the Magi. Then what was said through the prophet Jeremiah was fulfilled: "A voice is heard in Ramah, weeping and great mourning, Rachel weeping for her children and refusing to be comforted, because they are no more."' (Matthew 2:16–18)

The story has changed over the years, but the idea remains the same: God comforts Rachel and says that this sacrifice is not in vain and that her children will return to her.

When German aircraft bombed the city of Coventry in 1940, the local choir sang 'The Coventry Carol' about the women of Bethlehem and their murdered babies. This carol is one of the oldest English carols, dating back to the fourteenth century, and has survived by sheer luck, having been written down in 1534 by a local craftsman, and a copy made just before the original was destroyed by a fire in the Birmingham library where it had been kept.

The Ukrainian carol 'Ne Plach, Rakhyle' is also one of the oldest in Ukraine. It can be dated from its melody which is a variant of the Portuguese–Spanish Renaissance dance, *folia*, although how it reached Ukraine is unknown. The version which we know today reproduces the main melodic line of 'La Folia' (sonata number twelve in D minor from Opus No. 5) by Arcangelo Corelli.

The journey of this carol did not end in Ukraine. When Ukrainian peasants reclaimed Siberia and other Russian lands in the nineteenth century, it came with them to Ural and beyond: the furthest eastern point where folklorists have recorded it is Irkutsk.

Another group of people for whom this carol had resonance were political prisoners. From the time of the Polish uprisings of the nineteenth century to the end of the Stalinist camps, prison camps stretched from west to east in a long line. For them, 'Don't Weep, Rachel' took on a different meaning. In the latest version, this carol begins with a reference to the famous Old Testament tragedy of the Jewish people and ends with a direct parallel to the destruction of the Ukrainian people and innocent children by a Herod-like communist regime: 'Love for Ukraine – is all their fault, all their fault ...'

Sadly, this story continues to have relevance today. It is about tyrants – about their cruelty and, at the same time, powerlessness. It is

about the suffering of the weakest – children, women, elderly people, exiles – and has a deep meaning, for they will never be forgotten.

It is also a story with a socio-political dimension. This was well conveyed by Provost Howard of Coventry Cathedral in his sermon on 25 December 1940, given from the ruins of his cathedral after the German bombings: 'We are trying to banish all thoughts of revenge. We are going to try to make a kinder world.' This is a vision of the world not as it is, but as it should be.

The European community grows out of Judeo–Christian traditions and emphasises the values and dignity of every human life, regardless of status and origin. This community should root these values around the world instead of breeding aggression and colonialism, world wars, authoritarianism and totalitarianism, indifference to the weakest and to our neighbours, aggression towards strangers and exiles, and a tolerance for dictators. These traits are not unique to European

civilisation; they are woven through all countries and all periods of history throughout the world. But modern Europe, or, more broadly, the modern West, is a global power and must therefore bear global responsibility for the current state of the world.

All that remains is to weep with Rachel, or, together with the carollers, to believe that her story has an enduring meaning. Our victory is not guaranteed. It is possible that our short-term victories will be overturned and we will have to start all over again. But we will not give up. Our suffering must not mean we harden our hearts, and we will continue to try to make the world a better place.

The last two hundred years have become a new chapter in the history of carols, with some ironic and unexpected twists. Since Anglo-Saxon popular culture has become global, English carols are now heard all over the world. Some of them are borrowed and translated from other cultures, such as the Austrian 'Stille Nacht' ('Silent Night'). But thanks to this borrowing, they have become famous worldwide.

A perfect example of this is 'Shchedryk' ('Carol of the Bells'), the most famous Ukrainian carol in the world, best known in Mykola Leontovych's arrangement. It is a *shchedrivka*, that is, it has no Christian meaning. It originated in pre-Christian times and is not actually a Christmas song but a New Year's song heralding the beginning of spring, telling the story of a swallow's flight.

We do not know how this *shchedrivka* originally sounded or what it was called. According to one version, Leontovych heard it in Ukrainian Podolia, according to another – in Ukrainian Volyn. His first

arrangement was performed in 1916 in Kyiv, but its rise to worldwide fame is connected with the Ukrainian national revolution.

Despite having fought several armies at the same time, the young Ukrainian People's Republic suffered from a lack of international recognition. So Ukrainian leaders came up with the idea of sending a Ukrainian choir abroad under the direction of Oleksander Koshyts. The Ukrainian songs performed by this choir were to serve as an advertisement for the Ukrainian cause, and cultural diplomacy was to replace political diplomacy.

The choir went on a three-year tour, visiting ten European countries. They were heard by the American impresario Max Rabinoff,

who in 1922 invited the choir to perform in New York City at the famous Carnegie Hall. Before the end of the first act, the choir performed 'Shchedryk', and this performance received rapturous applause.

In a review of the concert, the *New York Times* wrote that Ukraine's music 'suggested the colossal wealth of youthful and untouched vitality which had tided over centuries of the most tragic history in the world.'

An American composer of Ukrainian origin, Peter Vilguski (Petro Vilkhovskyi), heard the choir sing 'Shchedryk' and translated the song into English, calling it 'Carol of the Bells'. This version has been used an incredible number of times in advertisements and movies (the most famous being the André Champagne commercial and the Hollywood hit, *Home Alone*). The most unique performance was by a group of NBA basketball players who recreated the rhythm of the song by bouncing basketballs on the gym floor.

Although this carol became popular in the West, it was little known in Ukraine until after the fall of communism. Despite the fact it did not have Christian symbolism, the Soviet authorities still considered it religious. After making a long journey around the world, it was revived and 'Shchedryk' finally returned to its homeland.

In addition to global expansion, the recent secularisation of Anglo-Saxon culture has contributed to the fact that during the holiday period, carols are now heard everywhere: at concerts, on the radio, from loudspeakers in crowded malls embellished with sleighs, colourful packages and chubby grandfathers in red suits. They have become part of the cultural code of the modern secular world.

At the same time, in this secular world, most people don't have the opportunity to hear the Christmas message, except in those Christmas songs played through speakers. While each song interprets the story of Christ's birth in its own unique way, many of them still retain the invisible link between the holy and the pagan, between angels singing over the hills beyond Bethlehem and a world simply celebrating joy in the midst of winter.

In anticipation of Christmas and the holiday itself, Christian families certainly sang these hymns, passing on their heritage, writing them into their own history. Even when families could not give their children the same education we have nowadays, they still managed to give them a basic knowledge; the children were brought up and educated at the family table.

But over time, in the cosy world that followed the Great War, when refrigerators and electric stoves became available to everyone, there was no longer the same need for family gatherings at a large dinner table. Comfortable housing became accessible for smaller families: people began leaving the communities where they had grown up, and moved to where jobs were being created. Spaces for a large family to gather at home were significantly reduced: the living and dining room, where several generations of relatives might have gathered to spend the evening reading, singing and talking by the fireplace, became silent. And yet, to this day, every Christmas Eve, when the shared dinner and the soft lighting of candles reappear on the table, and the familiar Christmas songs of childhood can be heard, the family returns.

Such a bright tradition has been preserved primarily in Central and Eastern Europe. However, the history of carols is different there than in the West. Communist and Nazi regimes, each for different reasons and motives, did not tolerate church carols. For the Communists, any religion was a relic and their intolerance of the carolling tradition was further exacerbated by the fact that it came from the 'hostile West'. For the Nazis, carols were reminiscent of the Jewish roots of Christ and his family. But since Christmas carols remained a popular folk genre, both communists and Nazis tried to take advantage of their popularity for their propaganda. For this reason, in the texts of former Christmas carols, Christian images and symbols were changed so that in the USSR they acquired a communist message and, in Germany, a Nazi one.

Today, the majority of people in the Western world know the words of the most popular carols and can sing them. But this does not mean that they believe in Christ. Christmas in the West has retained its festive mood, but, particularly since the 1960s when theologians started to talk about the 'Death of God', it is no longer a celebration of the birth of the Son of God. Christmas songs have become highly commercialised. Their number grows every year and it is rare that a rock or pop star has no Christmas song in their repertoire. Only a small proportion of these relate to gospel events or could be tentatively called 'Christmas' songs.

Yet there are still areas where the Christian Christmas has not been completely eradicated by communism or commercialised by capitalism. One of them is Galicia within the former Austrian borders – that is, parts of current Ukraine and Poland. The Galicians were lucky, at least in the fact that communism came to them later than to the rest of Ukraine as a result of the Second World War and being annexed by the Soviets. Those who want to hear carols or learn to sing them can still go to Lviv or Krakow, or better still, to a Galician town or mountain village where Christmas remains almost the same as a hundred or more years ago. But you'll have to hurry because commercialisation is already reaching these parts, too.

In the end, it is up to each of us to preserve or abandon the tradition of carols. There is, however, hope that the caring people of the world do not diminish in number. The appeal of the Christmas carol is as contagious as ever, bringing an incurable warmth and joyfulness to all who experience it.

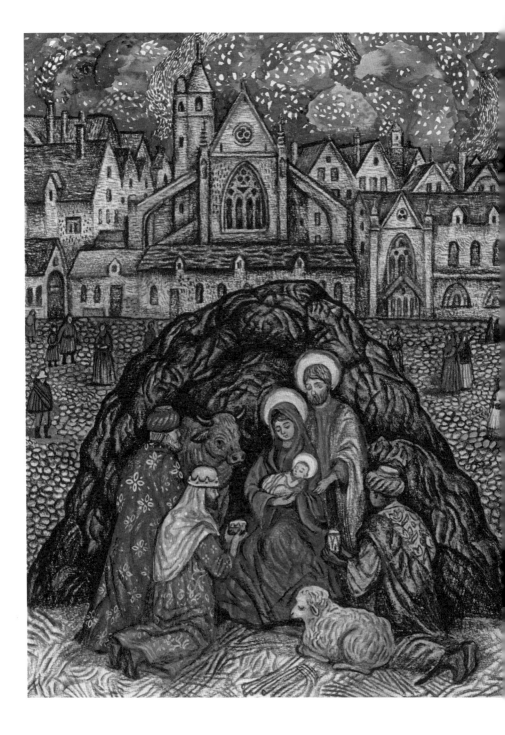

Vertep: The Nativity Scene

Among the symbols of Christmas there is one that breaks records in the number of names and meanings it is given. In almost every language it sounds different: *nativity scene* in English, *Krippe* in German, *kerststal* in Danish, *crèche* in French, *presipio* in Italian, *belén* or *pesebre* in European Spanish, *naciemento* in Central and South American Spanish (except in Puerto Rico, where it is called *portal*), *jeslicky* or *Putz* in Czech, *szopka* in Polish, *betlehem* or *születési jelenet* in Hungarian, *betleika*, *viartep*, *ostmeika* or *zhlob* in Belarusian and *vertep* or *shopka* in Ukrainian.

The nativity scene can vary in size from an eighty square-metre house (*Diorama Einsiedeln* in Switzerland) to a small box that fits under a Christmas tree or on a table. The smallest nativity scenes are made in the shell of walnuts, but in addition to wood and nutshells, materials such as dried melon (in South America) and paper (in the Czech Republic) are used.

The nativity scene shows figures from Christmas scenes: the baby Jesus, the Virgin Mary, Joseph, the Three Kings – and the largest can contain up to a thousand or more figures. If these figures are life-sized, live oxen and donkeys, sometimes sheep, are added to them. Since the 1990s, in Dublin the nativity scene has become a zoo for local farm animals, so that city children can see them at least once a year. Neither Luke nor Matthew mentions animals in Christmas stories, but since Christ was born in a stable or cave, it is reasonable to assume that there were animals at his birth.

The donkey is normally featured because it is likely that he carried Mary on his back to Bethlehem and was near the manger during the birth of Christ. The ox is not in the New Testament, but usually features to confirm the prophecy of Isaiah – that a donkey and an ox will worship the newborn Messiah (Isaiah 1:3). Sheep are also featured in Christmas stories, as the shepherds were among the first to come to greet Christ.

The Apocrypha (non-canonical Gospels) and legends added other animals to the Christmas story. The stork allegedly covered the manger with its feathers, so became the patron saint of newborns (hence, the belief that storks bring babies). The nightingale received the best voice among the birds for singing to little Jesus while He was sleeping. The youngest of the camels carrying the Wise Men and their gifts groaned with fatigue, and little Jesus thanked him for making him immortal. Therefore, among Christians in the Middle East, a camel still brings gifts to children for Christmas.

It is said that the spider hid Mary, Joseph and Jesus from the Roman soldiers with its web; the birds warned the Holy Family when the threat was approaching; the deer fell to its knees when it saw a star in the sky;

and that the bees sing the hundredth psalm at Christmas, but only a pure heart can hear this singing.

Due to the special role of animals in Christmas stories, it is believed that they should be treated with special kindness during the festive season. St Francis, who is said to have been able to converse with animals and birds, prayed for their salvation, assuming that they too had a soul. He placed an ox and a donkey in one of the first Christmas nativity scenes and urged Christians on Christmas Day to give cattle more food and sprinkle grain in the streets so that the birds could have plenty to eat. The tradition of being especially kind towards cattle at Christmas has been preserved in many nations. In particular,

the Polish add wafers (liturgical bread) to cattle food, and Ukrainians fill the manger with grain.

Sometimes the nativity scene is built without Jesus and he appears there only on Christmas Eve at exactly the time of his birth. In Italian nativity scenes, there is a hospitable shepherd, Jelindo, who allegedly let the Virgin Mary and Joseph stay the night on their way to Bethlehem. In the nativity scenes of Provence, one can see several figures – a seller of chestnuts or greens, a woman who sells fish, and a craftsman who sharpens scissors. In Catalonia, among the figures of the nativity scene is a peasant or soldier, Kagener, with his pants down, obeying the call of nature; it is believed that this figurine averts misfortune and symbolises the productivity of the land. A Mexican nativity scene may have figurines of a rooster, turkeys, fish, and women making tortillas. Peruvian ones often include a llama.

Nativity scenes are set up in various places: at the front of the church, in the central squares, near the municipalities. In South America, the nativity scene replaces the Christmas tree: families gather around it to pray, sing carols and exchange gifts. In Hungary, Poland and Ukraine, nativity scenes are carried from house to house by carollers. In some Muslim countries, nativity scenes are placed in apartment or shop windows to show that the owners are Christians.

The nativity scene can depict a stable or cave (in Slavonic, 'nativity scene' means 'cave'). In some nativity scenes, this cave or stable is transformed into a castle or royal chambers, symbolising that Jesus is the king of all nations. In Polish *shopkas*, a cave or stable is depicted as a cathedral. Banksy made his own version of the nativity scene, in which a hole from a shell in the wall can be seen above the figures of the Holy Family; his nativity scene is set in The Walled Off Hotel near the West Bank barrier that separates Israel from Palestine.

Nativity scenes can be static, with fixed figures, or mechanical, with moving figures. The largest mechanical nativity scene is in the Czech town of Jindřichův Hradec. It has 1,389 figures and holds a Guinness World Record.

Another version of the nativity scenes are puppet theaters, which show Christmas scenes, followed by short humorous performances on daily topics. Such nativity scenes are like dolls' houses with two floors: the upper floor representing Heaven and being used for the sacred Christmas scenes and the lower floor representing Earth and used for plays on household themes.

Nativity scenes can also consist of live performances on Christmas themes, with non-professional actors, adults, children or students. The most widespread theatrical form of the nativity scene – in the form of both puppet and living theatres – is found among the Slavic peoples, especially Belarusians, Serbs, Croats and Ukrainians. In addition to the Holy Family, the Three Kings, angels, shepherds, the devil, death, Jews, soldiers, cossacks and King Herod may appear.

Versions of the play may be different, but the plot is more or less the same: angels announce the birth of Jesus Christ, King of the world; King Herod is trying to find out where the Christ child is; he asks the Three Kings who refuse to betray the secret; and people try to deceive Herod. Not knowing where Christ was born, Herod then orders his soldiers to exterminate all the babies and when Herod seems to have succeeded and calmed down, death comes to him, removing his crown and head with a scythe; then the devil takes Herod to hell.

At the end everyone sings a carol together and wishes happiness, health and prosperity to the owner of the house and his family.

Time determines who should be in the nativity scene and who should not. Herod in Ukrainian nativity scenes can be Stalin, Ukrainian President Yanukovych, or Russian President Putin. The appearance or disappearance of certain figures is not whimsical – the nativity scene is both temporary and timeless. Hence, in every culture and in every age, the figures and figurines of the Holy Family are depicted according to the national circumstances of the time: in the Bavarian *Krippe*, Jesus is depicted as a well-fed child and the shepherds look like Bavarian Bauers; in South African nativity scenes, the Virgin Mary is black, and so on.

Whatever the forms of the nativity scene, they all have their origin in one place and time, and in one person: St Francis of Assisi. Born c1182 into a very wealthy family, he renounced the riches of the world and lived with ordinary, poor people. Simplicity and poverty went hand in hand with illiteracy. None of the peasants read the gospels, and the liturgy was conducted in Latin, a language they did not understand. Therefore, on Christmas Day 1223, St Francis staged a play for the

peasants of the Italian suburbs where he lived, in which he and his brothers from the monastic order enacted live scenes from the gospels. These nativity plays were inspired by a Palestinian pilgrimage to the birthplace of Jesus Christ. The whole performance took place in a cave: in addition to the monks, a live ox and a donkey also participated.

Some historians believe that the nativity scene existed before St Francis, and he only popularised it. But these beliefs cannot be confirmed. The very nature of his Christian spirituality suggests that St Francis is a likely creator of the nativity scene. At a time when Italy was full of spiritual profiteering and materialism, it was the message of Christ being born in poverty, humility and simplicity that made St Francis so popular among the common people: Almighty God came into the world first of all to the poor and disadvantaged, and all the rich and powerful, indifferent to their troubles, will be punished – just like King Herod.

From Italy, the nativity scene spread throughout the Catholic world, in particular in North and South America, Eastern Europe and throughout the Polish–Lithuanian Commonwealth – among Orthodox Ukrainians and Belarusians. There is evidence that, as early as 1470, Bernardine monks in Lviv erected a nativity scene at their monastery.

The question remains as to where the eastern boundary of the nativity scene lies. It came to Russia quite late, as a Christmas puppet show, and here it was mostly associated with high culture. But, as Russian art critic Iryna Uvarova writes in her book *The Nativity Scene:*

The Mystery of Christmas, the Russian nativity scene cannot be compared to the powerful, truly national *vertep* tradition of Ukraine.

The theme of *vertep* has impregnated modern Ukrainian culture – it is difficult to find an outstanding figure who has not written at least one article or poem on the theme of the nativity scene. The nativity scene is featured in the works of Taras Shevchenko, Panteleimon Kulish, Mykhailo Drahomanov, Ivan Franko, Les Kurbas, Ihor Kalynets, Hrytsko Chubai, Dmytro Pavlychko and other distinguished writers. Not surprisingly, the celebration of the nativity scene became a manifestation of Ukrainian identity, especially in the context of the Russification and Sovietisation of Ukraine. In the Soviet Union, Christmas was strictly forbidden, firstly, as a religious holiday, and secondly, as a public holiday (public holidays in the USSR could only be official). Carollers who walked door-to-door with the *vertep* (mostly children and teenagers) were caught by the police and their parents were fined.

In the cultural conflict between the Soviet (particularly Russian-speaking) and Ukrainian identities, the unspoken discussion probably went something like this: 'We have brought you high culture, along with education and industry!' – 'What kind of culture do you have, if you don't even have Christmas and a nativity scene?!' Accordingly, when Ukrainian intellectuals organised nativity scenes in Kyiv and Lviv in 1972, the KGB classified them as a manifestation of 'nationalist sentiments'. One of the first manifestations of the nationalist revival in Lviv was the street nativity scene of the Lion Society in January

1989. It is not surprising that in current-day times, when the Russian–Ukrainian war continues in eastern Ukraine, Ukrainian volunteers come to Donbas with their nativity scenes, and Donbas separatists and Russian media call these nativity scenes '*Banderite*' (the Banderites are members of the Organisation of Ukrainian Nationalists).

Who will win the war between these Christmas traditions is a purely rhetorical question. Christmas is invincible, as is one of its greatest and most popular symbols, the Christmas nativity scene.

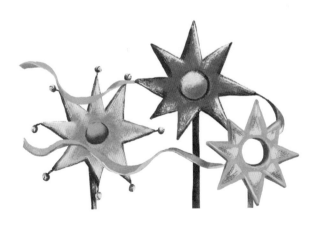

The Christmas Tree

I n Eastern Europe, the appearance of the Christmas tree is due
to German influences. The custom was brought to Polish lands
by German Protestants between 1795 and 1806. In the Russian
Empire, the first Christmas tree was introduced in 1817 by Tsar
Nicholas I at the request of his wife, the Prussian-born Princess
Charlotte. According to another version of the story, the Christmas
tree appeared in Russia a hundred years earlier, thanks to Peter I, but
the tradition did not take root.

Either way, from the mid-1840s, a real Christmas tree frenzy
began in St Petersburg, Moscow, Kyiv and other cities. At the end of
the nineteenth century, Chekhov ironically said that if this tradition
continued, there would soon be no forests left in Russia. But, as in
Germany, Poland and Russia, the tradition of putting up a Christmas
tree was limited to the richer and more educated classes. The Russian
Orthodox Church opposed this tradition because it considered it pagan
and German, and in 1916 they banned the Christmas tree as a German
symbol. In the villages, the role of the Christmas tree was played by

the *didukh*, a decoration made from a sheaf of rye, wheat, or oat, and ornamented. On Christmas Eve the *didukh* was brought into one's house and put on the holiday table or other prominent place. Bringing *didukh* into the home was considered the beginning of a great holiday.

We do not know when and where the tradition of putting up a Christmas tree came to Ukraine. However, we can safely assume that the emergence, as in other cases, was associated with German influences, because Lviv (known as Lemberg in German) was the largest city in Ukraine until the 1840s and was largely German. Throughout Ukraine, from Galicia and Volyn to the Black Sea coastal area, there were German colonies. It is probable, however, that in the western Ukrainian lands Christmas trees appeared in the villages in the 1920s and 1930s, and coexisted with the *didukhs*.

The Christmas tree spread to nations and countries that were not Christian. In the Soviet Union, the Christmas tree put in the Kremlin was the most important one. In Japan, in late December, many families decorate their homes with a Christmas tree, which in Japanese is called *Kurisumasu* (distorted from the English 'Christmas'). The Japanese took this tradition from the post-war American occupation of Japan, although the vast majority of Japanese people are not Christians.

Another attribute of Christmas – and the Christmas tree – is light. Christmas nativity scenes have a tradition of carrying an octagonal 'Bethlehem star' (in the Hutsul and Boiky regions, such a star is called a *vertep*). But festive candlesticks were deliberately *not* put in some churches in order to encourage parishioners to come with their lamps,

thereby reminding them that they are the light for the world; that the light does not remain locked in the church building, but must be with them wherever they go, especially in their homes.

In ancient Ukrainian tradition, a wax candle is lit on the table on Christmas Eve. And, according to the much newer tradition that Ukrainians acquired in the last century, they also turn on a flashing garland on the Christmas tree.

Light, according to a well-known saying by an unknown author, never fights darkness, but overcomes it with its very presence. Christmas does not fight hopelessness – it just comes, leaving no room for despair.

As the Christmas tree trend took off around the world, both its size and the size of gifts changed. At first, small Christmas trees were decorated and placed on the table, and small gifts were tied to the branches. But when the size of the tree grew, it moved from the table to the floor, and with it the gifts became larger, moving from the branches to being stacked on the floor.

The tradition of giving presents for Christmas was formed gradually. At first, these were handmade things – items of necessity rather than whims. In numerous books of different historical periods and localities, we come across mentions of such gifts for loved ones.

For example, warm mittens showed vital concern for the non-natives of the newly conquered American prairies; the *shopka* carved from alder was a shy confession of love for a violinist going on holiday to the Tyrolean Alps; knitted socks, handkerchiefs with embroidered initials, and crackers sent to the soldiers on the front line, along with letters about Christmas at home and how much everybody is looking forward to their return, gave them strength to continue their struggle.

Godfather Drosselmeyer's gifts to children in *The Nutcracker* story by E.T.A. Hoffmann reflects the era of ingenuity and prosperity and, at the same time, the deep desire of every child to learn not mechanics but a fairy tale. In Louisa May Alcott's classic story *Little Women*, modest but well-considered Christmas treats are given to the four March sisters, as well as to the poor family of German immigrants – a kind of declaration of the values of a democratic society. Henry van Dyke's *The Story of the Other Wise Man* features a sage who went with his friends to give gifts to the baby Jesus, but was held up on the way and gave each of the gifts to people who would otherwise perish, eventually leading him to meet the Saviour. And O. Henry's moving text, *The Gift of the Magi*, emphasises the value of naive devotion in an overly pragmatic world. At the same time, Christmas presents are a special symbol, even a prophecy: when the children in C.S. Lewis's *The Lion, the Witch and the Wardrobe* receive a sword, a bow and arrow, and a healing elixir from Father Christmas, they also accept their assigned missions in the battle against evil.

The culture of giving gifts for Christmas, popularised in the Victorian era, acquired a special meaning after the First World War. The gifts were not just expressions of courtesy, they told stories: 'we survived it', 'I'm glad you're back', 'thank you for waiting', 'this is our hope for a peaceful future and fulfilled dreams'. A destroyed Europe experienced the post-war Christmas with notable trepidation. Firmly convinced that this was the 'war to end all wars', Europeans saw Christmas as a symbol of hope for their own rebirth.

Traumatised by their military experiences, Europeans – both women and men, as well as their children – reached out to anything festive, as if it were medicine. The Christmas windows of shops and department stores turned into works of art, with exquisite electric light garlands, mechanical moving dolls and a generous variety of embellishments displayed like decorations on the stage of a theatre.

Generosity had always been considered a virtue, but was especially so after the war. What can now, in retrospect, look like the emergence

of consumerism, then seemed like a natural reaction to the times. People liked spending money, as well as what they spent it on and for whom. So even in societies that used to condemn extravagance, Christmas shopping was something completely different – an experience rooted in hope and love.

Children who, a few months or years ago, could have only dreamed of an extra piece of bread with jam, a pencil and notebook, or shoes without holes in them, now had the opportunity to fully enjoy the holiday, even if their parents did not have enough money to give them new things. A lot of activities were completely free – especially in stores, which no longer only sold goods, but also offered joyful

experiences. For example, in Britain, almost all major department stores had a Santa's grotto, and paying a visit became common pre-Christmas entertainment for children. The press printed photos of children with enchanted faces and wrinkled noses pressing to the windows of festively decorated shops. In the early 1920s, the *Evening News* in Britain even announced a competition for the best Christmas shop window display.

Even the exhausting Second World War could not destroy the pace with which new Christmas traditions developed. By the early 1950s, in countries where Christmas was not banned and renamed (or rebranded), Christmas decorations had already re-emerged in stores.

Due to commercial influences, Christmas as a phenomenon of economic magic extends to non-Christian countries too — especially to Japan where Christmas is about prosperity. However, this is not the

case for everyone. Because there is always a small number for whom Father Christmas does not put sweets under the tree. Instead, he puts in their hands a sword, bow or a bottle of healing liquid in order that they may join the army of the one who, as C.S. Lewis wrote, came to Earth disguised as a child, so that even the world's longest winter would not be left without Christmas.

St Nicholas and
Grandfather Frost

very Ukrainian child knows that St Nicholas brings Christmas presents, yet no one knows very much about him. The earliest account of this saint appeared several centuries after his death, but it is hard to separate fact from fiction.

He is believed to have been born in 270 in Patara, a port city on the southwest coast of modern-day Turkey. From there, he made a pilgrimage to Egypt and Palestine, and upon his return became Bishop of Myra, the capital of one of the eastern Roman provinces. As a bishop, he saw Christianity transformed from a forbidden religion to the official religion of the Roman Empire. In his early days as a bishop, under the reign of the Roman emperor Diocletian (284–305), Nicholas suffered brutal persecution and imprisonment. He was released when Emperor Constantine (305–337) came to power and legalised Christianity. Nicholas was probably one of the members of the First Council of Nicaea in 325, where the Creed was adopted, although his name is not found in the list of bishops present there. He died in Myra in 343 at the age of seventy-three.

The rest of what we know about St Nicholas comes from legends, two of which are particularly famous. The first tells of three poor sisters who had no dowry so could not marry, and Nicholas secretly threw three sacks of gold through their window at night. In the second legend, Nicholas went to a tavern and discovered its evil owner had killed three students and marinated them in a barrel, intending to use them as meat. Nicholas resurrected them and was thereafter considered the patron saint of students and children, as well as unmarried women, sailors, coopers, prostitutes and converted thieves.

Nicholas became a saint across the lands of the Byzantine Empire that had converted to Christianity (that is to say, the Orthodox world). In particular, he was considered the patron saint of Greece and Rus. It is likely that the oldest Ruthenian church (Ruthenian is the old word for Ukrainian), the church of St Nicholas in Kyiv, was named in his honour.

His appearance in the Catholic world was a consequence of his hometown being conquered by Muslim Turks in 1071, after the Battle of Manzikert. Given the danger that Christians would no longer have access to his tomb, St Nicholas's relics were stolen by Italian sailors and transported to the Italian city of Bari. It is said that these relics emit a fragrant myrrh, which is called the manna of St Nicholas. In 2009 the Turkish government asked the Italian government to return the saint's relics to Myra (modern-day Demre), the city where he was a bishop and where he was buried, but Italy is in no hurry to return its saint.

According to custom, a saint was honored not on his birthday, but on the day of his death – the day he was born to eternal life. For St Nicholas, this was 6 December according to the Gregorian calendar, or 19 December according to the Julian calendar. At first, this day was not directly related to Christmas, but from the twelfth century, it began to be treated as a harbinger of the Christmas holidays. From this time on, St Nicholas Day became a tradition: a day when gifts for children appeared under pillows or Christmas trees or in stockings hanging from fireplaces. That, of course, was provided children were well-behaved: if not, then sticks would be left. However, though St Nicholas sometimes left gifts and sticks at the same time, no one remembers an instance when he only brought sticks. In his great kindness he could not leave any child without a gift. The tradition of children writing letters to St Nicholas developed, in which they promised to be well-behaved, and in return asked for a gift. These traditions began in Italy and from there, spread throughout medieval Catholic Europe.

However, after the Protestants abolished the veneration of all saints, the cult of St Nicholas survived only in the Netherlands. There he was called *Sinterklaas*. On the night of 6 December, *Sinterklaas* would sail from Spain with his assistant, the Moor, *Zwarte Piet* (Black Pete), mount a white horse, and jumping from roof to roof, throw candy through the chimneys, which would fall directly into the shoes and stockings left by children. And *Zwarte Piet*, crawling through the same chimney, would put presents by the bed. The Dutch tradition of white people dressing up as *Zwarte Piet* with black faces is highly controversial. Protests against the practice have led to recent changes in the traditional *Sinterklaas* parades in the Netherlands.

It was from the idea of St Nicholas bringing gifts to children that Santa Claus was formed. This myth grew in the West from New York, which was originally a Dutch colony called New Amsterdam – the name Santa Claus is an Anglicisation of the Dutch name *Sinterklaas*. In this way, Nicholas was the only saint of the Catholic Church to survive in the Protestant world. He adds to the Christmas holiday magic and makes it especially appealing to children, returning them on Christmas Eve from the noisy streets to the family hearth.

The first non-Native Americans were quite secular in their views, but were fans of the Christmas holiday traditions from their Dutch and German homelands and continued to celebrate Christmas. New Amsterdam was probably the perfect place to give birth to the new

Christmas hero, Santa Claus, who embodied nostalgic folk traditions and secularism as well as the influences of various branches of Christianity – not to mention consumerism, which was also gaining momentum. The modern American Santa Claus has little in common with St Nicholas, except for having inherited his name. You only have to look at their images to see the difference: St Nicholas is depicted as a thin and grey ascetic with a serious expression, whereas Santa Claus is always smiling, rosy-cheeked and with a distinct belly.

Further east, the tradition of writing letters to St Nicholas and receiving gifts from him took root in lands that were under Catholic influence. This was especially true of western Ukraine. Here, St Nicholas Day became a favourite holiday for children, and for a whole year the saint was eagerly awaited. Children all over Ukraine would try not to fall asleep in order to catch a glimpse of St Nicholas delivering their presents. And the greatest disappointment of childhood was the discovery that St Nicholas did not, in fact, exist and that the gifts were brought by parents. The older children could feel superior to the younger children: only babies still believed in St Nicholas! At the same time, the first year that St Nicholas did not bring a gift for them was a sign that their childhood was over. Happily, though, even some adults remain children in their souls and do not stop giving each other gifts.

In contrast, in the Russian Empire in the early twentieth century, and later in the USSR, St Nicholas was replaced by Santa Claus. Then, after the fall of communism, St Nicholas returned to the Orthodox world, ousting Santa Claus. But the Santa Claus tradition showed no

sign of dying out, especially in Russia and Russian-speaking regions. The children who receive gifts twice benefit from this the most: from St Nicholas on 19 December, and from Santa Claus on 1 January.

St Nicholas was not the only one who brought Christmas presents to children. In England, this role was played by Father Christmas; in France by Père Noel; in Germany by Kris Kringl (*Christkindl*, 'Christ the Child', is not Christ himself, but more like a magic fairy); and in Italy by Babbo Natale.

In Italy, gifts are also brought by the good witch Befana. But, unlike Babbo Natale, she does not do it on Christmas Eve, but on the eve of Epiphany (5 January). Her name comes from the word 'Epiphany' (Orthodox Christians call this holiday *Vodokhreshche*, or Jordan). Unlike Babbo Natale, Befana flies on a broom, but, like Zwarte Piet, goes down the chimney and leaves gifts for the good children and a bag of ashes for the bad ones.

According to legend, Befana was sweeping in her house when the Three Kings passed by. They invited her to go with them to Bethlehem,

but she refused because she wanted to finish cleaning. She later regretted her decision, and since then, Befana has wandered the world, doing good deeds in an attempt to rid herself of the curse imposed on her. Once a year, she secretly visits the homes of every child and stares into their sleeping faces, hoping to find the baby Jesus among them.

In German folklore, Befana's counterpart is Frau Berchta. The *World Encyclopedia of Christmas* claims that the same figure exists in Russian folklore, under the name of Babushka (Grandma). But this is probably a mistake: the image of Babushka as Befana's Russian counterpart is a late literary invention, which appeared in a children's book written by Russian immigrants, published in the United States in 1960.

In Spain, on 5 January, the eve of the Three Kings' Day, gifts for the children are brought by the Three Kings themselves. They come on horseback or on camels delivering the presents to the homes of children as they sleep. In Greece, this role is sometimes performed by St Basil (Bishop of Caesarea Cappadocia, 329–379), whose day of veneration falls on 14 January (and, according to the Julian calendar, coincides with the New Year).

It is commonly thought that the Soviet government did not tolerate religion and religious symbols, and therefore replaced St Nicholas with the soviet invention of Did Moroz (Grandfather Frost). This is only half true: the Soviet authorities did replace St Nicholas with Did Moroz, but they did not invent him.

The origin of Did Moroz, like most icons of Christmas and New Year, is shrouded in a mist of uncertainty. Some say he originates from

Slavic pagan mythology and was called Koliada, the god of winter. The big problem with this story, however, is that we have no proof that such a god really existed in Slavic mythology. The only text that mentions Koliada is the *Husiatyn Chronicle*, a history of Ukraine written in the seventeenth century, at a time when Roman Catholic influences were quickly spreading through Ukraine. It is possible that the author of this chronicle translated the Latin calendar with a Slavic spin, and thus invented Koliada. Unfortunately, very few texts from Rus are left, so we know much less about it than we do about any kingdom in ancient Egypt, and we know less still about these pre-Ruthenian, so-called Slavic pagan times. It suffices to say that those who speak of the existence of Koliada in Slavic mythology also quote *The Book of Veles*, which claims to be an ancient text detailing Slavic history and religion, but is a well-known literary forgery.

The nineteenth century was the golden age of such fakes. It was a time of nationalism, and each nation invented its own traditions. The image of Did Moroz, as we know it, is associated with German nationalism. At that time, German nationalism was a revolutionary liberation movement and had little in common with Hitler's Nazism. The image of Did Moroz appeared on the eve of the Revolution of 1848, when German liberals tried to unite Germany – including the Austro-German lands – under democratic slogans.

The creator of the image of Did Moroz was the Austro-German artist Moritz von Schwind. In 1847 he illustrated a satirical poem by his compatriot Hermann Rollett about the adventures of Mr Winter

(Herr Winter). In von Schwind's drawings, Mr Winter is depicted as an elderly man with a long grey beard, in a hooded cloak and with a Christmas tree under his arm. On Christmas Eve, he goes from door to door and asks to spend the night, offering a Christmas tree in gratitude for hospitality. But everyone tells him to go away from the house – whether they are stingy peasants, wealthy burghers or nobles. They all celebrate Christmas with a festive table, gifts, singing and dancing, but none of them remember or understand the true spirit of Christmas. The story of Mr Winter is very reminiscent of Charles Dickens's *A Christmas Carol*. However, unlike Dickens's story, it does not have a happy ending – the fate of Mr Winter was prescient of the fate of a united and unhappy Germany.

Around the same time, Morozko, the Russian prototype of Did Moroz, appeared. Morozko is the evil spirit of the winter forest, turning

all who meet him into ice pillars. This is exactly how Moroz appears in Nikolay Nekrasov's poem 'Moroz, Red Nose' (1864): a poor peasant-widow, Daria, goes to the forest for brushwood, but unfortunately, she meets Moroz there and he freezes her to death.

In 1873 Russian playwright Alexander Ostrovsky wrote the play, *The Snow Maiden*, featuring incidental music by Tchaikovsky. It was based on a fairy tale about the unhappy love between a forest spirit-girl and the village shepherd called Lel. As soon as the Snow Maiden learns to love, her heart warms and she melts. In the play, Moroz is the Snow Maiden's father, who rushes to her aid. The play was relatively unsuccessful, until 1882 when it was staged as an opera by the Russian composer Nikolai Rimski-Korsakov. The scenic design for the opera's premiere was created by Russian artist Viktor Vasnetsov, and the costume design for Moroz was painted by Roerich. In this way, Did Moroz can be seen as a work of Russian secular culture, created at the time when Russia was inventing its national traditions.

Did Moroz became Russia's secular national hero, a replacement for its religious patron, St Nicholas. He became a tradition in the families of secular intellectuals, while among most Russian believers, including the peasantry, St Nicholas remained the main Christmas icon.

Hence, the Bolsheviks did not invent Did Moroz, they simply introduced him to their secular culture. But not immediately: Did Moroz remained out of favour with the communists, who considered the celebration of Christmas and New Year a bourgeois holiday, until the 1930s. He was reborn in 1935 with the lifting of the New Year ban and underwent a further metamorphosis: the Snow Maiden morphed from being his daughter into his granddaughter – and Did Moroz began to look increasingly like Santa Claus.

Like most symbols of Christmas and New Year, Did Moroz has absorbed various images from different cultures, including St Nicholas, and has become responsible for delivering gifts to children. From Soviet Russia, the image of Did Moroz spread into all the folk cultures of the USSR – even those peoples who knew neither frost nor snow and have never been Christian. He travelled to communist satellite countries in Central Europe, such as the German Democratic Republic, but with the fall of communism and the unification of Germany, he then disappeared from East Germany.

Today, Did Moroz remains popular in post-communist Russia and other former Soviet republics. But in the countries that have turned away from communism, such as the Baltic countries and Ukraine, Did Moroz has been driven out by St Nicholas. And so we are witnessing a cultural war between these two icons. The future of Did Moroz depends on the future of Russia: if it ever becomes a normal democracy, it is possible that Did Moroz, like the Snow Maiden, will melt away.

A ban on Christmas

Marx called religion 'the opium of the people', and the Bolsheviks were militant atheists. Everything relating to Christianity was subject to prohibition and repression. An unusual photo of Moscow in the 1920s shows a rally of small children campaigning for the abolition of Christmas. They are holding a poster in their hands that says: 'Parents don't confuse us, don't celebrate Christmas and put up a Christmas tree.'

But the 1920s were relatively peaceful times. The main attack on religion began during the so-called 'Great Leap Forward' of 1932–3, as socialism forcibly took hold. Not only Christmas, but all holidays were removed from the official Soviet calendar. This was done by a special resolution of the Soviet government in 1930, which abolished all holidays and introduced a six-day working week. Instead, non-working days were introduced on the 6th, 12th, 18th, 24th and 30th of each month. The 'Great Leap Forward' was to lead to the building of a single country, the USSR, and the spread of socialism throughout the world.

Just as the Bolshevik communists tried to create their own traditions for the formation of new revolutionary citizens, the Nazis tried to reformat German religious holidays according to their ideological needs. With Hitler's rise to power in 1933, the warmth of the nativity was transformed into a celebration of the solidarity of the Aryan race and loyalty to the Führer.

The Nazis were particularly annoyed by the image of Christ as a Jewish child and Mary and Joseph as Jewish parents. As a result, Christian symbols of Christmas were to be replaced by pre-Christian Nordic ones. Christ was replaced by the Aryan god Odin; the Holy Family, ox and donkey in German nativity scenes were replaced by the image of the ancient German forest with deer and hares; the Christmas tree was decorated with a swastika instead of a Christmas star; and carols such as 'Stille Nacht' ('Silent Night') were rewritten so that there were no Christian images and symbols. The performance of carols in their original Christian version were interpreted as a manifestation of political disloyalty.

How successful were these Nazi attempts to 'nationalise' Christmas? On the one hand, there were Nazi organisations, especially among women and children, such as The Hitler Youth, who fought aggressively against the Christian signs of Christmas. But, on the other hand, during the entire period of Nazi rule, there were voices of protest from the Catholic and (to a lesser extent) Protestant Church. Of course, there were also Catholic priests and Protestant pastors who pretended not to notice the anti-Christian nature of Nazi rule (especially Nazi attacks on

Christmas) and supported the Nazis, particularly during the war. But between these two extremes were a large number of German people who could not, and did not, want to give up Christmas as a Christian holiday and continued to celebrate it as before. The effectiveness of Nazi propaganda declined as reports of German defeats came from the front.

In 1935, Stalin announced that socialism in the USSR was mostly built and that 'life has become better, life has become happier.' On 28 December 1935, the central newspaper *Pravda* published a letter from the second secretary of the Communist Party of Ukraine (and one of the organisers of the Ukrainian famine) Pavlo Postyshev calling for a beautiful Christmas tree to be put up for children. In pre-revolutionary times, he wrote, the bourgeoisie and bourgeois officials had put up Christmas trees for their children, decorated with colourful toys for the New Year, and the children of workers had stared enviously at the merriment of the rich through the window. Why should Soviet schools, orphanages and nurseries deprive Soviet children of this pleasure? The condemnation of the Christmas tree as a bourgeois relic must be stopped, and the boards of Soviet institutions, together with Komsomol members, must make the Soviet tree shine in all cities and collective farms.

Such a letter could not have been written without the consent of his superiors. According to one version, Stalin's daughter, Svetlana, was invited to celebrate Christmas at the British Embassy in Moscow. She returned very excited by what she had seen, especially the glass ornaments and candles on the Christmas tree, and began to beg her father to lift the ban on the Christmas tree and give back to the Soviet children the joy of the winter holiday. According to another version, one of the Soviet leaders, riding in a car with Stalin, complained that Moscow was very grey, and noted that it would be good to allow Muscovites to have Christmas lights and Christmas trees. Stalin liked the idea, and he ordered such an 'initiative'.

One way or another, in 1936 the New Year was officially restored. However, 1 January remained a working day – it was only declared a holiday after the war, in 1947. The Soviet New Year was to replace the Christian Christmas. For this purpose, Santa Claus was introduced (instead of the pre-revolutionary St Nicholas) and he was joined by his assistant, the Snow Maiden. The Christmas octagonal star was replaced by a red pentagonal one. Carols were revived, but their words were rewritten in a new way, so that Lenin took the place of Christ, and the words 'new joy' were replaced with 'new Council' (meaning Soviet power) and so on.

The people would pay for celebrating Christmas by losing their documentation certifying that they belonged to the communist party. This was a terrible punishment at the time, because anyone expelled from the party under Stalin became an 'enemy of the people' and banned from many aspects of normal life.

Of course, the best way to illustrate Christmas in the USSR is through real stories, but often it is not easy to read them. Memoirs of the 1930s and 1940s are full of scenes of violence and cruelty, showing

the fall and rise of the human spirit. The Gulag prisoner, Polish writer Gustav Herling-Grudziński, wrote of how even the 'mortuary' – a place where 'last-leggers' were sent for a slow death in the camp – became festive on Christmas Eve. The doomed prisoners greeted each other with eyes red from tears: 'All the best – next year at large', although 'at large' meant not true freedom, but death.

In another story from a post-war Christmas Eve, students in western Ukraine were returning from the villages by train to the university in Lviv because they could be expelled for not attending lectures during religious holidays. There was no light in the carriages, so someone started singing, 'A New Joy has Come'. After the first carol, someone timidly began the second one, 'Have you Heard, People'. He was joined by others: 'Our mother Ukraine has been shackled'.

Suddenly, a man's voice was heard from the middle of the carriage: 'Shut up!' Someone began nervously lightning a match near the benches, but the guys behind him blew it out. At the first stop, the man ran out of the car and returned with a lantern and an NKVD representative (People's Commissariat for Internal Affairs): 'Who started this?' The boys shrugged their shoulders: 'We don't know... It was dark, and there are a lot of people, you see.'

The power of traditional Christmas carols also shines through in the story of Ivan Kozlovsky, said to be Stalin's favourite singer. Former Soviet Foreign Minister Andrei Gromyko recalled that, 'When some members of the Politburo began to loudly express their wish for Kozlovsky to sing a merry folk song, Stalin said calmly, but in a way that everyone could hear: "Why put pressure on Comrade Kozlovsky? Let him perform what he wants. And he wants to perform Lensky's aria from Tchaikovsky's opera *Eugene Onegin*."

Everyone laughed, including Kozlovsky. He immediately sang Lensky's aria. Everyone was pleased with Stalin's humour.'

It would be futile to try to imagine the singer as a victim of Stalin's whims – Kozlovsky spoke of Stalin with respect that bordered on admiration for his understanding of music. But the question is: what would Kozlovsky have sung if he had had a choice?

He gave the answer at a jubilee concert held at the Bolshoi Theater in Moscow on 18 January 1970, in honour of his seventieth birthday. In Ukraine, this is the day of the second Holy Supper, when carols are performed again, and Kozlovsky would certainly have known that. In his memoirs, he wrote that he had grown up on Ukrainian songs and as a child had gone to sing carols every year.

When Kozlovsky gave the jubilee concert, it was in the era of liberalisation in the USSR after Stalin's death. A year or two later, new arrests would take place in the Soviet Union, which later became known as the 'Great Pogrom'. But Kozlovsky could not have known that, and, in the end, as a two-time Stalin Prize winner and someone who had achieved everything in life, he had nothing to fear. So in the last part of the concert Kozlovsky began to sing carols. At first, he sang 'The Wonderful Star is Coming'. Then, 'Herod the King Pursued Christ', 'Good Evening to You, Sir', 'A New Joy has Come' and 'News has Spread all Over the World'. The concert ended with the singing of 'Mnohaya Lita' ('Many Years'), and it is said that Kozlovsky came down from the stage and walked through the hall scattering the audience with wheat from the village of Maryanivka in the Kyiv region where he had grown up.

The most extraordinary fact of this story is that a recording was officially released by the Soviet record company 'Melody'. The album consisted of four records, with the carols on the 'B' side of the last album. This was the first and only time that Ukrainian carols in the USSR were performed publicly and without censorship. Not only was the record not banned but it was even released twice: the first time in 1970, immediately after the anniversary, and the second time in 1974. Like every good product in the USSR, it was sold under the counter through good connections.

Typically, the Soviet Union would take a folk song, change the words in it so that it sounded communist, and present a new version as folk art. For example, in the Ukrainian carol 'Good Evening to You, Sir' there are the words, 'Oh, rejoice, earth, the Son of God has been born.' In the Soviet version, this line became: 'Oh, rejoice, earth, Lenin has been born.' But at the anniversary concert Kozlovsky sang this carol properly – with 'Son of God'. Ivan Kozlovsky may have been Stalin's favourite singer, but he sang in God's way.

After Stalin's death in 1953, party leaders began recording New Year radio messages. In the 1970s, it became a tradition for people to celebrate the New Year crowded around their televisions, which by then had become widespread. On 31 December 1970, Secretary General of the USSR Leonid Brezhnev congratulated viewers on an 'unforgettable year' in the first televised New Year address. Finally, 'Soviet champagne' became cheaper as production was automated. In 1986, US President Ronald Reagan greeted Soviet people for the first time on television, and Soviet Secretary General Mykhailo Gorbachev addressed the Americans.

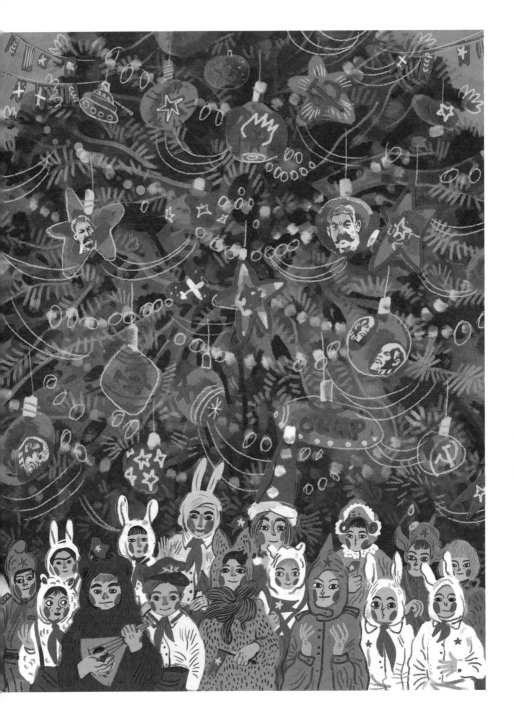

Christmas Truces

Christmas awakens solidarity even among enemies. It unites even those people who on other days prefer to look at each other through the sight of a machine gun. It also brings a warning to every government that, like Stalin's, believes it is in power for good: Herods do fall.

The beginning of the First World War was accompanied by patriotic demonstrations and the belief that the war would be short, and that by Christmas the troops would return home victorious. Military realities quickly dispelled this illusion – the war lasted a long time. Neither side had a decisive advantage and, despite the bloody battles, the front line moved very slowly, often stuck in one place for weeks, if not months. As British officers ironically said, if the war continues at this rate, it will take 180 years for the army to reach the Rhine.

From as early as the autumn of 1914, an impromptu truce began on several parts of the Western Front. It peaked on Christmas Eve, when the frost hit and the trench swamp turned into a slightly more tolerable frozen ground. The German Kaiser ordered 100,000 Christmas trees to be sent to the front to raise the fighting spirit of the soldiers. But they had the opposite effect. They reminded German soldiers of the warmth of the family home at Christmastime.

On Christmas Eve, the Germans began to sing Christmas carols. As the trenches were fifty to a hundred metres apart and the frosty air carried the sound well, their singing could be heard on the other side of the front, and British soldiers began to respond with their own carols. Some carols, such as 'Stille Nacht' ('Silent Night') and 'Adeste Fideles' ('O Come, All Ye Faithful'), were known in both languages, so they were an ideal tool for international communication. After the singing, there were Christmas greetings from both sides. The next day, on Christmas Day, instead of shooting at the enemy, the soldiers fired into the air; they met on neutral ground and exchanged food and souvenirs; they tried to understand each other. As it turned out, many German soldiers worked in Great Britain before the war, so fortunately knew basic English.

There were rumors that British and German soldiers even played football together, but senior officers allegedly ended the match by ordering to resume fire and punishing the soldiers who joined the game. In a version of the story by the British poet Robert Graves

published in 1962, the Germans beat the British by three goals to two, but only because the referee, an Anglican priest, showed too much Christian charity and credited the Germans with an offside goal.

The episode of the Christmas football match is immortalised in monuments in Britain and France. To many, the idea of this Christmas truce seemed unbelievable, especially as the war dragged on, and in most cases, the soldiers did not play football with their enemies, but with each other, and none of them were punished.

The fact is, however, that the Christmas truce of 1914 was joined by about 100,000 soldiers and officers on both sides. There were also attempts at reconciliation outside the front. British women suffragettes sent a Christmas letter 'To the Women of Germany and Austria', and Pope Benedict XV called on both sides to 'silence the guns along the front line at least upon the night when the Angels sang' – but this initiative was rejected by officials.

It has been suggested that when soldiers celebrated Christmas at the front, they may have known of a similar precedent, almost fifty years old at the time, from the Franco–Prussian War of 1870–1. On Christmas Eve 1870, the bells of the local church rang in a small town near the front line, and the soldiers on both sides, without collusion, stopped the fire and began to sing carols. The next morning the fighting resumed.

But Christmas 1914 remains unique. In 1915–7, there were isolated cases of a Christmas truce on the Western Front, but as command became increasingly centralized, none were as large as in 1914.

Truces also took place on the Eastern Front, between Bulgarian and Greek Orthodox soldiers, and most famously in Przemyśl, where an Austrian military unit defended a local fortress from Russian troops. On the night of 25 December, Austrian troops ceased fire, and Russian troops did the same. A poster 'We wish you, heroes of Przemyśl, Merry Christmas and we hope we can reach a truce as soon as possible' was hung on the Russian side, and then soldiers from both sides met in neutral territory and exchanged gifts. The same thing happened on Orthodox Christmas, two weeks later.

During the Second World War, such truces were impossible. Firstly, both sides were at war to destroy each other, and secondly, celebrating Christmas in the Red Army was unthinkable. However, in the memoirs of Nata Lenko, there is a mention of one episode from the early post-war years, when the Ukrainian Insurgent Army (UPA) soldiers ('Banderites') in Zakerzonia (ethnic Ukrainian territory within post-war Poland) arranged a truce with the Red Army soldiers: 'On Holy Evening, in one of the houses, Banderites and the Red Army accidentally meet face to face. The former were already sitting at the table when the latter came in. Instead of shooting, one invites others to the table. After dinner, the Soviet officer wants to thank them for their hospitality and offers the rebels his pistol. They refuse: it is not proper for a soldier to be without a weapon.'

Maybe there were more such instances, but in any case, the Christmas truce of 1914 was a bright episode in the history of twentieth century European wars. Christmas truces were possible in old, Christian Europe,

where the warring parties were guided by the Church's call to avoid bloodshed during major Christian holidays. In this sense, the truce of 1914 was the last glimpse of an ancient chivalric ethos.

The Christmas truce of 1914 blossomed in post-war mass culture – in films, such as *Joyeux Noël* (2005) and music, such as Paul McCartney's song 'Pipes of Peace' (1983). And this is not by chance. Post-war Europe is built on the principle of 'Never again'.

Unfortunately, world history teaches us that war is the rule and peace is the exception – tyrants die and tyrants are born; violence spreads and innocent people are murdered. However, the exception must be remembered and upheld so that it becomes the new rule. In times such as the people of Ukraine are living through today, the Christmas story has particular resonance. God sent a vulnerable child to the world to bring peace, reminding us that genuine peace should also embody justice for the poor, the weary and the oppressed. The victims of war must be remembered and the tyrants must fall. Peace is worth fighting for and must be preserved. There is hope for that in the mystery of Christmas.

A note on the cover

While working on the cover of the book *A Ukrainian Christmas*, most of all I wanted to make it festive. The plant and flower motifs, as well as ornaments have an in-depth history in Ukrainian art. They were created both in happy times and in times of war and grief, and it helped Ukrainians to maintain their identity and preserve their memory. It is very much in tune with the holiday of Christmas and the birth of a new life. No matter what.

Olena Staranchuk

About the illustrators

Olena Staranchuk created the cover design for this book. She is a graphic designer, illustrator, co-founder, and curator of the Pictoric Illustrators Club in Ukraine since 2014. Olena received a scholarship from the Minister of Culture and National Heritage of the Republic of Poland, 'Gaude Polonia'. She has won the 'Best Book Design' award, 2018-2020 and collaborates with Ukrainian and European publishing houses.

Julia Tveritina (@yuliiatveritina) is a graphic artist, painter, and illustrator, most famous for her war diary illustrations. She was born in Kyiv, Ukraine, in 1986 and holds a master's degree from the National Academy of Arts and an Assistant-Internship at the National Academy of Arts. Julia received a grant from the President of Ukraine for young artists in the fine arts and, in 2015, received a silver medal from the Ukrainian Academy of Arts and Ministry of Culture for the best master's diploma work in graphic techniques. She won the 'Best Book Design' award in 2018 for the book *Girls Pover* in Mystetsky Arsenal, together with Anna Sarvira. She worked on the illustration course at Suzhou University, and participates in numerous international exhibitions. Julia has had more than twenty solo exhibitions.

Lusya Stetskovych (@lusya.stetskovych.illustration) is a children's book illustrator based in Lviv, Ukraine. After gaining a master's degree in Graphics from the Ukrainian Academy of Printing she worked as a 2D artist in game studios, and as a graphic designer, before eventually transitioning into illustration. Lusya has worked with publishers and private clients for the last nine years.

Yuliya Nesmeyanova came into book illustration after a long period of working in an animation studio. She enjoys combining different materials in illustrations and creating collages. She believes that modern technical capabilities make it possible for artists to bring to life their most daring fantasies, and to integrate all sorts of unexpected materials into their work.

Kateryna Borysyuk was born in 1992 in Ukraine. She has a master's degree from the National Academy of Arts and currently works as an art teacher and book illustrator.

Picture credits

About the authors

Yaroslav Hrytsak is a Ukrainian historian and public intellectual. Professor of the Ukrainian Catholic University and Honorary Professor of the National University of Kyiv-Mohyla Academy, Professor Hrytsak has taught at Columbia and Harvard Universities and was a guest lecturer at the Central European University in Budapest. He is the author of many historical books, including several bestsellers and the recipient of numerous national and international awards. He has written opinion pieces for many publications including *The Times*, the *New York Times* and *Time Magazine*, and lives in Lviv, Ukraine.

Nadiyka Gerbish is a Ukrainian writer, translator, and human rights advocate. She has written nineteen books, many of which have become bestsellers and have won numerous awards. A number of Nadiyka's children's books are studied in schools in Ukraine and have been published in braille and audiobook to be used in inclusive education programmes. She works as a Riggins Rights Management European rights director and lives in Ternopil, Ukraine.

Acknowledgements

I belong to a group of Ukrainian historians who believe that rethinking the Ukrainian past is a necessary precondition for Ukrainian success. The broader the historical context the better, and a global context is best of all. One way to reveal Ukraine's history is to focus on the history of war and revolutionary violence. Ukraine has been a geopolitically important borderland, and what was going on in Ukraine during 1914–1945 had an impact on global developments – as does the current Russia–Ukraine war. To that effect, I wrote a global history of Ukraine that covered this dimension of Ukrainian history. There is, however, another, more peaceful and joyful way to rethink the Ukrainian past in the global context – and that is to focus on the history of Ukrainian Christmas. After all, Christmas is one of the most global events – probably, *the* most global event. This book is my first attempt to explore this entanglement between Ukrainian history and the rest of the world, and it is hopefully not the last. I would, however, never have dared to take this initial step without the encouragement of two people: Olena Khirgii, the director of the Portal publishing house who published this book originally, and Nadiyka Gerbish, my co-author. Without them, this book would never happen. I would like to thank them for their support and help, and for creating the best parts of this book!

Yaroslav Hrytsak

My first memories of Christmas begin with my grandfather. Christmas was his favourite holiday, and would make his kind, sad eyes sparkle with boyish joy. He kept reminding me that I ought not lick the *makohin* if I did not want my future husband to be bald. I kept doing just the contrary right in front of him, with a defiant look in my eyes. I knew he admired that. Coming from a family that had been resisting communism in the most intricate of ways, he encouraged all the disobedience and mischief in me, calling it 'freedom'. I still have a childhood photo of me sitting on grandpa's lap with a wooden *makohin* in my hand, and his eyes full of laughter. He died more than twenty years ago, but I've never lost those vivid memories of him and the Christmas joy that he ignited in me as a child.

When Olena Khirgii, one of the founders of Portal publishing, invited me to write a book about Christmas together with the Ukrainian rock (a.k.a. history) legend Yaroslav Hrytsak, I didn't have to think twice. Christmas always comes with presents, and the friendship that has stemmed from this co-authoring will be a cherished lifelong gift.

When the brutal war was brought to our country, one thing made it possible for us not to surrender but to fight and believe in victory – the spirit of freedom and resistance, nurtured in the homes and tables of Ukrainian families that chose to celebrate Christmas, a holiday banned by the vicious Soviet regime. I would not be writing this text today from my Ukrainian home if it weren't for the courage and sacrifice of the Ukrainian soldiers and volunteers. And it would not be possible to continue our struggle without the tremendous support of our allies.

Catherine Burke, the publisher of Little, Brown, was the person who decided that Ukraine must be present not only in the Western press, but also in Western bookshops and libraries. I am deeply grateful to Cath for all her hard work and heartfelt encouragement. I answered some of her letters while the air-raid sirens were wailing, and thought then that, thanks to this visible chain of resistance in the face of the ongoing Russian invasion, our current suffering is not in vain, and there is still hope even in the midst of the greatest crisis.

I am incredibly grateful to Helen Brocklehurst, the editor who made the English text flow so smoothly. She was the one who untangled all the unsolved mysteries with her thoughtful questions, kind inspiration, and good humour.

Marta Gosovska and Anastasiya Fehér from Ukraine performed a Christmas miracle by translating the text with incredible speed, in the hottest days of summer.

The cover artist Olena Staranchuk added a candle and a wheat ear to the design – two symbols that speak of Christmas Eve traditions and the current history of Ukraine. The candles lit in memory of the murdered Ukrainians, and the wheat burned, bombed, and stolen by the Russian army.

I am grateful to the team of brilliant professionals working on this title at Sphere, especially Sian Rance, Sarah Kennedy and Abby Marshall. To all our readers who do not remain indifferent. To the people of Ukraine who choose not to give up – even now, when the present is painful, and the future is uncertain. Among them are my grandmother and my mother-in-law, who taught me to cook different types of *kutia*. And my mother, who has been celebrating Christmas for most of the past fifteen years with orphans and single mothers in Kenya, and has been teaching them to sing the beautiful Ukrainian *kolyadky*.

Most of all, I am thankful to my husband Igor and my daughter Bogdana, with whom even the most ordinary supper feels like a Christmas Eve.

Nadiyka Gerbish